for my mother and father
Suey Ting Yee and Seow Hong Gee

# DREAMS
# IN HARRISON RAILROAD PARK

### POEMS BY
### NELLIE WONG

Kelsey St. Press

Some of the poems in this book have been published or will be published in the following magazines:

POETRY FROM VIOLENCE, EAST/WEST CHINESE AMERICAN JOURNAL, Ms., WOMEN II

ISBN 0-932716-14-8
Book Design by Marina LaPalma and Karen Brodine
Illustrations,  page 15      Florence Wong
                page 23      Lai Chop
Photograph,   page 45      Raisa Fastman

First printing: 1977
Second printing: 1978
Third printing: 1981
Fourth printing: 1983

# CONTENTS

# GRANDMOTHERS' SONG

Grandmothers sing their song
Blinded by the sun's rays
Grandchildren for whom they long
For pomelo-golden days

Blinded by the sun's rays
Gold bracelets, opal rings
For pomelo-golden days
Tiny fingers, ancient things

Gold bracelets, opal rings
Sprinkled with Peking dust
Tiny fingers, ancient things
So young they'll never rust

Sprinkled with Peking dust
To dance in fields of mud
So young they'll never rust
Proud as if of royal blood

To dance in fields of mud
Or peel shrimp for pennies a day
Proud as if of royal blood
Coins and jade to put away

Or peel shrimp for pennies a day
Seaweed washes up the shore
Coins and jade to put away
A camphor chest is home no more

Seaweed washes up the shore
Bound feet struggle to loosen free
A camphor chest is home no more
A foreign tongue is learned at three

Bound feet struggle to loosen free
Grandchildren for whom they long
A foreign tongue is learned at three
Grandmothers sing their song

# HOW A GIRL GOT HER CHINESE NAME

On the first day of school the teacher asked me:
What do your parents call you at home?

I answered: Nellie.

Nellie? Nellie?
The teacher stressed the l's, whinnying like a horse.
No such name in Chinese for a name like Nellie.
We shall call you *Nah Lei*
which means *Where* or *Which Place.*

The teacher brushed my new name,
black on beige paper.
I practiced writing *Nah Lei*
holding the brush straight, dipping
the ink over and over.

After school I ran home.
Papa, Mama, the teacher says my name is *Nah Lei.*
I did not look my parents in the eye.

*Nah Lei? Where? Which Place?*
No, that will not do, my parents answered.
We shall give you a Chinese name,
we shall call you *Lai Oy.*

So back to school I ran,
announcing to my teacher and friends
that my name was no longer *Nah Lei,*
not *Where*, not *Which Place*,
but *Lai Oy, Beautiful Love*,
my own Chinese name.
I giggled as I thought:
*Lai Oy* could also mean *lost pocket*
depending on the heart
of a conversation.

But now in Chinese school
I was *Lai Oy*, to pull out of my pocket
every day, after American school,
even Saturday mornings,
from Nellie, from *Where*, from *Which Place*
to *Lai Oy*, to *Beautiful Love*.

Between these names
I never knew I would ever get lost.

## LIKE THE OLD WOMEN SUGGESTED

A girl is bathed in mustard,
then in oatmeal.
(Like the old women suggested).

She is scrubbed until the water runs red.

Still
the girl can't eat crab,
wear a dress
or play with boys.

She plays hooky from gym
and sleeps in the school solarium.
Her skin is her crutch.

She stays under the covers,
imagines her skin is cream.
It is her toy,
her itching, her temporary
relief.

Once her skin becomes cream,
she will be ready for market.

## CHICKEN SOUP

A woman stands over the stove stirring a pot of chicken.
The chicken is steaming in its whole skin.

The woman's daughter enters the kitchen
and puts a bag of rice on an oiled teak chair.
She whispers to the woman:
Elder Sister, I will eat with you tonight.

The woman continues to stir the pot of chicken.
Her forehead is unlined.   Stuffed bitter melon is arranged
on a platter of dragons and clouds.
She hoists the chicken onto a chopping board
and slices the wings and legs
as she has done it all her life.

The woman thinks to herself:
The rice will be fluffy tonight
no matter who I am,
no matter what I am called

Before the ancestral altar she places
two dishes of chicken breasts, two cups of wine.
She says to her daughter:
We must feed your father
and we must feed your mother.
Then we can eat.

The two women sit in their usual places.
They drink their soup, white of green onion floating on top.
The only sounds,
    chicken bones snapping.

## WHERE ARE YOU, MAMA?

Are you here, Mama,
or are you asleep
in a valley of that
orange moon?

Do your cheeks shine?
Does your gold tooth sparkle
in a field
of white daisies?

I stand here in frayed pants.
Will my sister turn up
with needle and thread?

My gloves slip from my hands.
Must I wear them
even if they are only
black gauze?

Will you come, Mama,
on some cloudless day
and let me eat strawberries?
I will find a fork
somewhere.

## IRONING

Papa drank and ate
while I ironed my family's clothes.
In our silence he blurts:
"Marriage, hmphh!"
I did not answer Papa's words.
I only ironed my family's clothes.

## UNDER COVER

Mama covered our heads
with scarves.
Tied them like shoestrings
we couldn't unlace.

Our hair, once thick and glossy,
now short stubbles,
ready for execution
in our own neighborhood.

Just girls who played
in the dirt, shot
each other with foxtails,
arrows to the spine.

Played house, Gorilla,
Kick the Can.  Hid from men
who wet their lips, snapped
their fingers, plucking time.

Mama said we couldn't be seen
like this, lice
sucking blood
from her daughters' heads.

How she burned incense
at the temple, pleading.
Our hair washed
not often enough.

If the neighbors asked,
she would say
best to keep
the girls' hair short.

How she explained
the scarves in summer,
indoors, remained
her secret.

## CAN'T TELL

When World War II was declared
on the morning radio,
we glued our ears, widened our eyes.
Our bodies shivered.

A voice said
Japan was the enemy,
Pearl Harbor a shambles
and in our grocery store
in Berkeley, we were suspended

next to the meat market
where voices hummed,
valises, pots and pans packed,
no more hot dogs, baloney,
pork kidneys.

We children huddled on wooden planks
and my parents whispered:
We are Chinese, we are Chinese.
Safety pins anchored,
our loins ached.

Shortly our Japanese neighbors vanished
and my parents continued to whisper:
We are Chinese, we are Chinese.

We wore black arm bands,
put up a sign
in bold letters.

# CONFESSION

I dream,  I dream
I steal a child, its eyes
yellow lights
filtering
dark roots
in my garden

I have to confess
my act.
Thievery,  is it?


It is your child,
I return it
while pile drivers
outside my window
hammer,
hammer

# DREAMS IN HARRISON RAILROAD PARK

We sit on a green bench in Harrison Railroad Park.
As we rest, I notice my mother's thighs
thin as my wrists.
I want to hug her
but I am afraid.

A bearded man comes by, asks for a cigarette.
We shake our heads, hold out our empty hands.
He shuffles away and picks up
a half-smoked stub.
His eyes light up.
Enclosed by the sun he dreams
temporarily.

Across the street an old woman hobbles by.
My mother tells me:   She is unhappy here.
She thinks she would be happier
back home.
But she has forgotten.

My mother's neighbor dreams
of warm nights in Shanghai,
of goldfish swimming in a courtyard pond,
of having a young maid
anoint her tiny bound feet.

And my mother dreams
of wearing dresses that hang in her closet,
of swallowing soup without pain,
of coloring eggs
for an unborn grandson.

I turn and touch my mother's eyes.
They are wet
and I dream
and I dream
of embroidering
new skin.

# HOW THERE IS ANGUISH

How there is anguish not knowing light,
how the dark feeds moderation,
a tightrope walker in fear of height.
How the outdoors mean a reprieve,
ducks eating from gnarled hands.
What birds there are I cannot name.
Leaves beneath my feet might be eucalyptus.
How there is relief between muslin,
dreams sliding a child in a park,
how a fall incites her tears,
the pain of unknown matter.

How the light means learning to iceskate
and fall, swim and possibly drown
in pools deceptive as magicians.
How doors are mirrors beckoning touch,
electric, silver.

How I sense the danger in light,
the clarity, how I recede into darkness,
jumping rope on the sidewalks of childhood,
tackled in touch football,
falling, falling
from the sun's harsh glare.

## JEWELRY AND THINGS

I like jewelry as much as my sisters,
my mother who is gone.

I smile when someone compliments
my jade donut embellished with gold,
jade heart or five-dollar gold coin
necklace, my lapis lazuli ring
purchased one spring vacation
centered with Persian turquoise.

When someone asks if my ring
is imperial jade, I refer them
to books and museum catalogs.

Seven days I rotate my pieces
like deciding which flavor to try
of Bud's ice cream.

As if I entrust my immortality
in mudware figurines
of three Chinese ladies, a San Antonio
wedding dress hand-embroidered
with pink and orange flowers,
a lamb suede jacket from China,
grape goblets found in antique shops,
ivory chopsticks with my father's name,
a teak hope chest carved
with spring blossoms, tiny birds,

still I think of oranges,
small pyramids of them
on plain white plates
purposely placed on mantels,
on tables and especially
in the kitchen god's domain.

I like to think
I don't beseech idle gods
like my mother and my grandmothers
who I never knew, wanting to trust
in the fragility of jade
knowing, believing
without heirs
the heavens
will forget me.

If only I could forgive myself,
I could enjoy jewelry and things
for their own sake.

# NOT FROM THE FOOD

Once I organized a dinner
for office friends
and I was proud when I ordered
barbecued spareribs, eggroll appetizers
bird's nest soup
empress chicken with asparagus
peking duck and thousand-layer buns
lobster cantonese
mushrooms, grass, black, button
yang chow fried rice
sweet and sour rock cod
oolong tea
fortune cookies
and almond delight
and I was prouder still
when I invited my guests
to tour dark alleys
the sing-song waves of faces
peeping from second-story windows
pointing to ducks, squabs,
thousand-year-old eggs
me on the perimeter
of Chinatown
with my office friends
gulping wine, holding my nose,
masked, playing oriental,
inscrutable, wise.
Now standing
before a brass spittoon
I recall that time
and I want to puke
not from the food, my friend,
not from the food

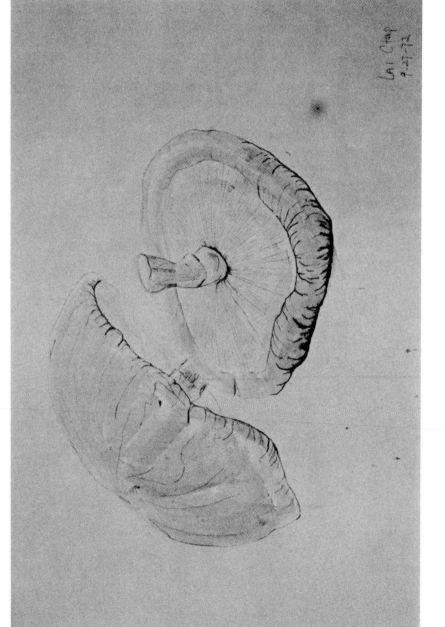

Lois Clap
2-27-72

# MAGAZINE POEM FOR FATHER'S DAY

A rare way to celebrate Father's Day?
Fragrance west of Colorado sage,
a "Male Tennis Player" figurine,
less work for father, a personalized deluxe,
half gallon pouring stand, easier to pour
his Chivas Regal, artifacts
by day, by night.

Say it with diamonds?  Gifted lighters,
smart investment in a 55-acre estate,
hang around with a Minolta, things
not so simple any more.  Soak up sun
on a rooftop pool, a man has the right.
Blend of ideas, making machines do more
so man can do more.  Cry a little,
laugh a lot among the ruins.

What does it cost to stay at the Ritz?  Enjoy deep sleep,
as a king, sensible affairs,
serene, push button remote control.
Carousel of grey flannel, got style,
ready for a new kind of Seville,
hassle out of traffic, tap the music,
accelerate to soft, tailored upholstery.

No place for rare taste,
kicking you upstairs
a figure of speech.  Really deep, deep
into the countryside, in brief
goings on about town
are oceans apart.
Technology, orange pekoe, the St. Tropez tan,
for emphasis the momentum
of big rigs.

Why go on?  Bag and baggage, breath
of spring, indulge without guilt
garden found floating
in racy deck shoes, in 4-wheel drives.

This not written for you, my father,
who sold mustard greens from a truck,
in your shorts somewhere,
your knees I laughed and loved.

## VOICE

What is hidden in morning glorys closed for the night?
Can't leaves be torn to find the veins?

Have birds forgotten, forgotten their legs need stretching?
Will it help if I offer you my lute,
some warm wine, my indelible pen?

And while some angels have abandoned their wings,
my voice not so much indigo, not so much new,
is something different.

And what of your voice, these slippers you wear?
Are they butter or leather?

In my dream, urchins of the sea form movable spines,
they detach themselves like sunstars on a new course

And my wish, no longer suspended,
finally comes home.

## PAINTING A ROOM YELLOW

Yellow as saffron the walls crack
memories green from warning, away
from molding.   How the light changes.

Floors the rawness of pine, not
puritan grey.   The ceiling bares
arrangements naked as skin.

The bedstead, one dusk pink, glosses
black, a newborn child
with thick, thick hair.

The woodwork maneuvers moths
from the garden, flies that cling
to the Victorian globelight.

The sky enters, inquisitive old tenant.
And like a bat, head hanging
downward, I listen to the moon rise.

## WOMAN IN PRINT

In the coffee shop I see a woman in a print dress.
It is 38 degrees outside, but she wears no coat.
She merely sits quietly,
alone
smoking a cigarette,
her gray hair combed back.

I have seen this woman, always coatless,
walking by a construction site.
I have watched construction men watching her
and I assume
she descends their darkened stairs.

She is as naked as any woman I have ever seen
or do my eyes deceive me
in this downpour?

I am a woman.

I wear a coat.

## WE CAN ALWAYS

A television comedian says:
"Women are no longer bobbing
their hair because
they are slanting
their eyes"

and people laugh

A television comedian says:
"Hi!   I'm Ruru,
fry me
to Frorida"

and people laugh

A disc jockey says:
"You should know better
than to rob
a Chinese grocer
If you do
you will want to rob
again in another hour"

and people laugh

A newspaper columnist says:
"How come them heathen Chinee
are always observing New Year's
a month late?   When they gonna
get up to date?"

and if we can't laugh
at ourselves, we can always
go back

## POEM FOR A TROLLEY BOY

from seeing the film
"Dodes-ka-den"
by Akira Kurosawa


Dodes-ka-den, dodes-ka-den,
you chant the song
of a trolley car.

You rise from the junkyard,
the technicolored garbage.
Rats with spaces between their teeth
wait and watch.

Wearing white gloves you go to work.
The sun is your mechanic,
you conduct, you build new tracks
on barren land.

Your mind is pure snow.
Fresh fallen, you scold the painter
sitting on your imaginary tracks.
Does he want to die, you ask.

Back home, beneath the soot of the city,
your mother prays to Buddha.
She chants, she chants,
her language is incense.

Wired to yourself,
you push, you pull.
Around you school children taunt,
beggars scoop uneaten fish
from back-alley kitchens.
Men drink, trade wives
while women gossip, beat
the family laundry, hang
their bodies out to dry.

Around you they undream
your world, trolley boy,
and you laugh noodles.

## POEM FOR A WOMAN WHO HAS FALLEN

You are there, sprawled, art deco
on the corner of 14th and Broadway.
The wind has not blown you there.
The stars have not guided you.
But you are there suddenly
a flash as my eyes search the street.

Other passers-by wait for their bus,
tap their toes, stare at the sky, moon
at dark leather boots
in shiny windows, see themselves
styling after tomorrow, a touch
of greenery, the flush in their cheeks.

I run to help you, are you okay?
One arm lifts yours and you say
you slipped.

Are you someone's grandmother?
Are you hungry?
What do you keep in your string shopping bag?
Do you have a transfer?
Do you live in a small room?
Do you cook oats on a hot plate?
Do you feed a sick husband?
Do you find it hard to go to the toilet?
Do you talk to yourself?
Are you your own friend?

I wait to cross the street, the light still red.
A man says to me:
"They don't make 'em nice
like you anymore."
He chucks my chin with a corner
of his newspaper.

And I imagine if I am lonely
the young man would buy me
coffee, a Miller's Hi-Life.
How impressed he seems
with me, a stranger
going home.

I scurry as the light changes.
I'm afraid to look over my shoulder, afraid
he will follow me, afraid
he will take
the same bus.

The No. 15 arrives, I hop
on, search for friends in faces
fuzzy as stars.
So many eyes are closed.

I'm glad I escape the young man
who might be a sailor,
I'm glad I escape the old woman, knowing
I can't be there
the next time she falls, knowing
what spills from her bag
will be crushed
by stampeding feet
hitching to safety
to the end
of the
line

## LOOSE WOMEN, YOU SAY?

Women who sit on bar stools?
Women who walk the streets?
Women who wear no girdles?
Women who see married men?
Women who drive trucks?
Women who shoot their lovers?
Women who kill their rapists?
Women who defend themselves?
Women who touch women?
Women who write about sex?
Women who smoke cigars?
Women who act in porn films?
Women who commit suicide?
Women who beat their children?
Women who go crazy?
Women who go underground?
Women who abort?
Women who flirt with men?
Women who paint their faces?
Women who stand up?
Women who show their teeth?
Women who fight in the ring?
Women who open their mouths?
Women who laugh out loud?
Women who say no?
Women who ride motorcycles?
Women who climb telephone poles?
Women who wear pants?
Women who run?
Women who divorce?
Women who spread their legs?
Women who fly?
Women who go out into the world?

## DRUMS, GONGS

Firecrackers pop
                drums    gongs
and here they come
parading in glittering cheong sam
slits    up their sides
their legs and thighs exposed
to leering eyes

They sway, they posture
these    American girls
whose ancestors landed years ago
some tutored in Cantonese
impressing red-eyed judges
in a four-hour show

They sing, they dance
ah    almond delights
their bodies ripple
undulating waves

Now the ritual continues
now the envelopes open
and firecrackers pop
                drums    gongs
and there she is
Miss Chinatown U.S.A.

She is crowned, she is furred,
she is highly glossed
and the search is over
Oh!  Let's show the world

Miss Chinatown U.S.A.
like no other
is real
is real
is real China doll.

## RELINING SHELVES

Can you imagine joy
in relining kitchen shelves?
In rows of tiny red tulips
splashed on yellow?
Ah, the grease, the grime
they play their part
nagging silently
each time you open
the doors for some oil,
a covered casserole.

And you wonder if the Chinese bowl
with pink peonies,
if the handthrown jar
with brown and gray waves,
if the yellow dish
with a crack in its belly
will meet with the Snowdrift,
collide with the peppercorns,
tackle the mustard,
ruminate with the rum abstract.

Do they creep out of the cupboards
at night, talk with the ants,
collaborate with the dust?
And instead of going to the beach,
I contemplate hours
at the Dime & Dollar
and reline the shelves.

Oh, kitchen of dreams,
you make the broom dance
the question of domesticity.
If I could eat
and sweep.

Meanwhile on the evening news
a girl testifies
she has been raped.
Did she resist?
Oh yes, she did,
she stood up
not even five feet tall
against her attackers
and her attorney admits
his client once had sex
with a woman
but in that case
she had been willing.

In a news article
a GI raps about Vietnam
how a prostitute was taken
like a sack of rice
from a GI's bed,
how the girl
had to be returned
to the first GI,
because the chick was his,
because the sergeant said so.

And I ask myself
what does relining shelves
have to do
with a girl who's been raped
who's had sex with a woman,
what does relining shelves
have to do
with a prostitute
who is called a "gook"?

## ON PLAZA GARIBALDI

The mariachi beckon, their guitars,
their violins string themselves,
me, striated
among the people.

Their smiles, their eyes plead for work.
No barrier this language.
I am their teeth.

Meandering I watch the fountain
gush promises in this twilight,
this scene.    This is truly Mexican,
someone told me.

Barbecued goat's meat, ears of corn,
platters of flan assault my eyes.
I am afraid.    My stomach has a mean streak.
I apologize for it.

A little girl tugs at my sleeve,
"peso, por favor?"
I want to gather her, smell flowers
but her mother is watching.

At the edge of the plaza
a young girl leans against a gray wall.
She is a donut, half raised.
The men who watch her
finger themselves
inside their pockets.

I tell myself:
I am not she, I am not she.
She is someone else's
sister.

## DAY OF THE DEAD

I open the door in my mask.
"What is that lady?" a little goblin asks.
And I might say I am surviving
the ghosts of myself.
And I might say I have only begun
to wear this suit of armor, my hair
aflame, my eyes blazing
beyond the bodies
of my unknown ancestors.
I fly a kite of a centipede,
flap its million legs,
land on the wings of a golden phoenix
calling me to a land
of hills and birds,
calling me beyond
my childhood fears.
And if I worship the dead,
it is because
I hear my parents whispering
through the marrow of my bones
asking to be fed.

# FROM A HEART OF RICE STRAW

Ma, my heart must be made of rice straw,
the kind you fed a fire in Papa's home village
so Grandma could have hot tea upon waking,
so Grandma could wash her sleepy eyes. My heart
knocks as silently as that LeCoultre clock
that Papa bought with his birthday money.
It swells like a baby in your stomach.

Your tears have flooded the house, this life.
For Canton? No, you left home forty years ago
for the fortune Papa sought in Gum San.
In Gold Mountain you worked side by side
in the lottery with regular pay offs
to the Oakland cops. To feed your six daughters
until one day Papa's cousin shot him.

I expected you to fly into the clouds, wail
at Papa's side, but you chased cousin instead.
Like the cops and robbers on the afternoon radio.
It didn't matter that Papa lay bleeding.
It didn't matter that cousin accused Papa
of cheating him. You ran, kicking
your silk slippers on the street, chasing
cousin until you caught him, gun still in hand.
My sister and I followed you, crying.

If cousin had shot you, you would have died.
The cops showed up and you told them how cousin
gunned Papa down, trusted kin who smoked
Havana cigars after filling his belly with rice
and chicken in our big yellow house.

Papa lay in his hospital bed, his kidney removed.
Three bullets out. They couldn't find the last
bullet. A search was made, hands dove into Papa's
shirt pocket. A gold watch saved Papa's life.

Ma, you've told this story one hundred times.
The cops said you were brave.  The neighbors said
you were brave.  The relatives shook their heads,
the bravery of a Gold Mountain woman unknown
in the old home village.

The papers spread the shooting all over town.
One said Papa dueled with his brother like
a bar room brawl.  One said it was the beginning
of a tong war, but that Occidental law
would prevail.  To them, to the outside,
what was another tong war, another dead Chinaman?

But Papa fooled them.  He did not die
by his cousin's hand.  The lottery closed down.
We got food on credit.  You wept.
I was five years old.

My heart, once bent and cracked, once
ashamed of your China ways.
Ma, hear me now, tell me your story
again and again.

## PICNIC

Each Sunday I climb the mountain to picnic
with my mother and father in their twin coats,
breathing air
that only the mountains can give,
air as fresh as carp swimming upstream.

These Sundays my mother and father and I talk.
Oh, how we talk and talk!
Of apples and lace and cloth bound books,
of sour plums that make our mouths water,
changing expressions on our putty faces.

Although we talk together, we three,
we promise each other nothing.  Not trees,
not oranges, not fish
for it is not our time to be fenced in,
not when spring promises its own
flowering quince.

I hold my mother's and father's hands tightly,
drinking the pools of their eyes.
It is strange we communicate now,
this way,
where there are no phones.

Together we celebrate the Tiger's Year.
We feast on chicken, mushrooms and the monk's dish,
pregnant with its cellophane noodles and fine black hair.
Our laughter is perfumed with incense
that the spirits drink.

We swim, drunk with the sea in our ears,
as seagulls swoop down to eat with us.
They are welcome guests and sit on my father's knees
which are still knobby and my mother is still
telling him what to do.

Look! The swallows are building their nests
and we toast what little ricewine is left.
The chrysanthemums bend their heads.
I gather fresh lichee and leave my mother and father
my only silk coverlet.

Nellie Wong was born and raised in Oakland, California. She works as a secretary in San Francisco and lives with her husband, Jim Balch, in Oakland. She is grateful to the feminist writers' group, The Women Writers Union.